HOW TO MAKE
LINGERIE

- WITH INFORMATION
ON STITCHES,
EMBROIDERY AND
FASTENINGS -

BY

ISABEL HORNER

British Library Cataloguing-in-Publication Data
A catalogue record for this book is available from the
British Library

Contents

DRESSMAKING AND TAILORING

Dressmaking and Tailoring broadly refers to those who make, repair or alter clothing for a profession. A dressmaker will traditionally make custom clothing for women, ranging from dresses and blouses to full evening gowns (also historically called a mantua-maker or a modiste). Whereas a tailor will do the same, but usually for men's clothing - especially suits. The terms essentially refer to a specific set of hand and machine sewing skills, as well as pressing techniques that are unique to the construction of traditional clothing. This is separate to 'made to measure', which uses a set of pre-existing patterns. Usually, a bespoke tailored suit or dress will be completely original and unique to the customer, and hence such items have been highly desirable since the trade first appeared in the thirteenth century. The Oxford English Dictionary states that the word 'tailor' first came into usage around the 1290s, and undoubtedly by this point, tailoring guilds, as well as those of cloth merchants and weavers were well established across Europe.

As the tailoring profession has evolved, so too have the methods of tailoring. There are a number of distinctive business models which modern tailors may practice, such as 'local tailoring' where the tailor is met locally, and the garment is produced locally too, 'distance tailoring', where a garment is ordered from an out-of-town tailor, enabling cheaper labour to be used - which, in practice can now be done on a global scale via e-commerce websites, and a 'travelling tailor', where the man or woman will travel between cities, usually stationing in a luxury hotel to provide the client the same tailoring services they would provide in their local store. These processes are the same for both women's and men's garment making.

Pattern making is a very important part of this profession; the construction of a paper or cardboard template from which the parts of a garment are traced onto fabric before cutting our and assembling. A custom dressmaker (or tailor) frequently employs one of three pattern creation methods; a 'flat-pattern method' which begins with the creation of a sloper or block (a basic pattern for a garment, made to the wearer's measurements), which can then be used to create patterns for many styles of garments, with varying necklines, sleeves, dart placements and so on. Although it is also used for womenswear, the 'drafting method' is more commonly employed in menswear and involves drafting a pattern directly onto pattern paper using a variety of straightedges and curves. Since menswear rarely involves draping, pattern-making is the primary preparation for creating a cut-and-sew woven garment. The third method, the 'pattern draping method' is used when the patternmaker's skill is not matched with the difficulty of the design. It involves creating a muslin mock-up pattern, by pinning fabric directly on a dress form, then transferring the muslin outline and markings onto a paper pattern or using the muslin as the pattern itself.

Dressmaking and tailoring has become a very well respected profession; dressmakers such as Pierre Balmain, Christian Dior, Cristóbal Balenciaga and Coco Chanel have gone on to achieve international acclaim and fashion notoriety. Balmain, known for sophistication and elegance, once said that 'dressmaking is the architecture of movement.' Whilst tailors, due to the nature of their profession - catering to men's fashions, have not garnered such levels of individual fame, areas such as 'Savile Row' in the United Kingdom are today seen as the heart of the trade.

LINGERIE

THOUGH the making of lingerie is not, technically speaking, dressmaking, the well-dressed woman will naturally see that her invisible garments are as dainty and shapely as her visible ones. However smart and becoming in themselves her frocks may be, their effect can be spoiled completely by being worn over badly-fitting lingerie. Paper patterns for underwear are modelled with as much care as those for upper garments, and should be selected quite as thoughtfully. Also, just as much care should be taken in their fitting and making, although the actual workmanship is simpler than in dressmaking, and a smaller equipment is needed.

MATERIALS

These should be light in weight and dainty in weave, though at the same time strong in texture and dye, in order to withstand the rigours of the laundry—unless, as so many women do, you wash your own lingerie; and even then some strain is unavoidable. So, when buying your materials, test them by pulling gently in both directions, and be sure that they are guaranteed fadeless, and also, in the case of woollens, unshrinkable. For "best" wear at its most luxurious there are georgette and ninon; when something less ephemeral is desired, silk, crêpe-de-chine, satin and rayon are available. (A good satin wears remarkably well, and is not really extravagant when its cost is balanced against its good qualities. Many a bridal gown of shimmering ivory satin has ended its career twenty years later as "nighties" and "knicks"!) For everyday wear lawns and cottons, either white or coloured, plain or patterned, are suitable, and may be most attractive. Broadly speaking, at the present time coloured fabrics are more favoured than white ones, though there are still many fastidious women who are faithful to fine white linen lawn trimmed with a little satin stitch embroidery or *broderie anglaise*, and perhaps a few real lace medallions. Others with similar tastes, though lighter purse, may use fine nainsook for everyday at least, with good crêpe-de-chine for slips and knickers. (Passée frocks of satin and crêpe-de-chine, either plain or patterned, can always be cut down into these garments.)

STITCHES

All stitching should be firm, in order to resist the strain of wear and washing; yet at the same time it should be as light as is consistent with strength, for clumsy stitching and coarse thread will prevent the effect of daintiness which is so desirable. Therefore strong but fine thread should be used in sewing, and both it and the size of the needles should be in keeping with the nature of the fabric. For all materials other than cottons fine sewing silk is unsurpassed, as it is more elastic than cotton, and therefore will not break so easily under strain. For white lawn or nainsook the thread may be no. 100, the needle no. 10 or 12, and the machine needle no. 11 or 12; for the same materials coloured mercerised matching cotton should be used, no. 40 or 50, with the same needles as before. For finer materials threads and needles should be proportionately finer, and, of course, sewing cotton or silk should always match in colour.

Some people consider hand sewing essential to the best class of work; but really, if the machining is done well and with a small stitch, there is no reason why the seams, at least, should not be done by machine, thus saving time and labour. Open seams, even with neatened turnings, are taboo; for, besides being untidy, they will not stand the strain of repeated washing. The seams most in use for thin fabrics are the French seam and the French fell, and in both of these the raw edges are enclosed. Run-and-fell seams are used only for the firmer materials, for which either of the previously mentioned seams would be too bulky.

FRENCH SEAM

How to make this is shown in Fig. 53, p. 103, and its making is described on p. 102. Each line of stitching should be pressed, and stretched slightly during the process (to counteract the tightening caused by the stitching) under a warm iron, before doing the next one. Remember in hand stitching to make every ninth or tenth stitch a back stitch for firmness.

FRENCH FELLED SEAM

This is even quicker to make than the previous seam, as it has only one row of stitching. It is illustrated in Fig. 54, p. 103, and described on the same page.

RUN-AND-FELL SEAM

Tack the two edges together on the fitting-lines on the wrong side, then stitch on the fitting-lines by machine from the side which will be on the top when the seam is finished, or from the under side if hand running is used. Cut off the under turning to 1/8 inch, or more if the material is a fraying one; then turn down the upper turning over the lower one as narrowly as possible, folding in the raw edge, and tack close to the fold. Stitch by machine close to the fold, or fell by hand. (See Fig. 27, p. 58.) Note that in side and shoulder seams the front of the garment should be felled onto the back.

BEADED SEAM

This looks very charming for thin fabrics, using silk beading for silk, or "near" silk, and cotton for cotton or linen. Beading generally has a strip of plain material with raw edge at each side. Lay the beading right side downward on the right side of the material with the corded edge close up to the fitting-line, then run the two together close up to the corded edge. (See Fig. 140, p. 262.) Cut off the turning of the material a few threads beyond the sewing, and cut off the turning of the beading a little wider. Now roll the beading turning over the material edge towards you, and while doing so apply whipping stitch, working this over and over towards you and pushing off the little rolls from the eye of the needle so that this is never taken really out until the seam is finished. (See Fig 151, p. 285.) If the beading has no turning, tack it up to the fitting-line as before described, then cut off the material turning and roll this over the beading edge with whipping stitch. Treat the other side of the seam in the same way, then press lightly with a warm iron. Lace beading, which has corded edges, may be applied similarly.

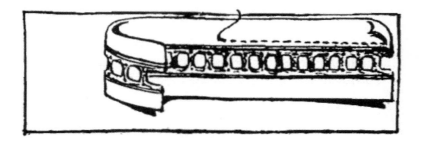

Fig. 140.—Applying Beading for Seam.

HEMSTITCHED SEAM

(by machine)

This can be done at any sewing-machine shop very cheaply, and is most satisfactory for very thin fabrics. Prepare the seams by laying one edge over the other and tacking through the fitting-lines, and the work will be returned to you with the hemstitching exactly over the tacking. (See Fig. 141A, p. 263.) Cut away the turning close up to the stitching on both sides, then press on the wrong side, stretching slightly at the same time. (Fig. 141B.) Be sure to tack with matching thread (silk or cotton, as the case may be), as the tacking-thread will be caught in with the machining, and cannot be removed. (It is usual to have any hems stitched to match, and how to prepare these will be described later.)

RULES FOR HEMS

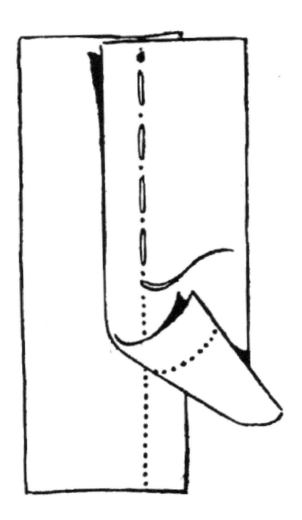

Fig. 141A.—Preparing Hemstitched Seam.

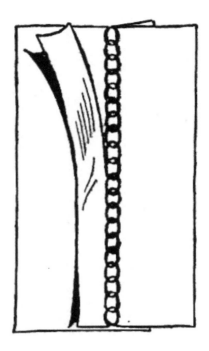

Fig. 141B.—Finishing Hemstitched Seam.

The depth of hems varies with their positions, On the bottom of a petticoat-slip or nightdress for instance, from 1/4 to 2 inches is correct, and other edges in proportion—according to fashion and the kind of material. As a rule the lower edge of these two garments is on the straight, or only very slightly curved, so that the tacking of the hem is an easy matter. In any case, the bottom of the hem should be turned first from the right side—one gets a better line that way—and tacked finely, close to the edge. Then on the wrong side the depth of the hem should be measured on the turning either with ruler, tape, or a notched card, and the turned-in edge tacked into place. If the edge is on a slight curve the resultant fullness on the upper edge should either be gathered finely or laid in small pleats to fit. The hem should be pressed lightly before being felled by hand with small stitches, taking up merely a thread of the outer material, with a double stitch at intervals on the turned-in edge for safety. If the hem is machined, it should be done from the right side as near the turned-in edge as possible, so that careful tacking is needed as a guide.

When a plain hem is used on transparent fabric, the turned-in part should be the full depth of the hem, so that it is three-fold.

A deep hem on a garment cut on the bias is not possible, and the lower edge may be finished with one not more than 1/4 inch wide, or with one of the hems described later.

IMITATION HEMSTITCHED HEM

(by hand)

This may be worked on ninon or any soft, fine fabric without drawing threads. Tack a hem from 1/8 to 1/4 inch wide. Take rather thick thread and a coarse, blunt needle. Join on at the left end of the hem, then put the needle under the fold and bring out 1/16 inch above.* Insert the needle in the single fabric close up to the fold and slightly to the right, so that the stitch produced is slanting; bring out the needle about 1/12 inch to the left in the single fabric (making a perfectly straight stitch on the right side of the material), then pass the needle under the fold again and bring out 1/12 inch from where the first stitch came out, and on the same level. Repeat from*. Pull the thread rather tightly so that rather large holes are made in the single material. (See Fig. 142.) Press on the wrong side.

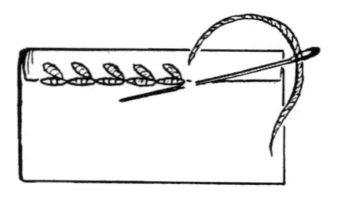

Fig. 142.—Imitation Hemstitched Hem.

HEMSTITCHED HEM

(by machine)

Tack the hem carefully, as for an ordinary plain hem, with the tacking as near the turned-in edge as possible, and using thread of the same colour as material, for the reason given in the instructions for a hemstitched seam. The finished stitch is the same as for the seam. When the fabric is transparent it is best not to turn in the raw edge of the hem, but to tack an even line 3/8 inch below the raw edge. The hemstitching will come exactly over this tacking, and the raw turning must be cut away above it. Press on the wrong side and stretch slightly.

ROLLED HEM

This is only suitable for very thin materials, but it has a very decorative effect. The whipping stitch is shown in Fig. 30, p. 58, and the making of the hem is described on p. 108. It should be worked on the wrong side with rather coarser thread than is used for the rest of the sewing.

CROSS STITCHED HEM

This also is for thin fabrics, and a fairly thick thread should be employed. (It is illustrated in Fig. 143.) Tack the narrowest hem possible, join on the silk or other thread (which should be rather coarse) at the right end, on the wrong side of the material. Then work over and over the hem with coarse but evenly-spaced stitches, bringing out the needle close up to the turned-in edge. When you get to the left end work back from left to right over the first set of stitches, crossing each perfectly. Do not pull the stitches tightly.

Fig. 143.—Cross Stitched Hem.

SCALLOPED HEM

This is only suitable for crêpe-de-chine and other thin materials. It is shown in Fig. 61, p. 109, and is described on the same page.

OTHER EDGE FINISHINGS

There are other edge finishings which cannot exactly be called hems, as they are more in the nature of trimmings.

BOUND EDGES

Either self material or one of contrasting colour or pattern may be used, but the strips must be exactly on the bias, and should be cut according to the directions given on pp. 68–9 (see Fig. 39, p. 69), and then sewn on in the way described on pp. 171–2. (If preferred, bias binding sold by the yard may be used.) When the material is very thin, the strips should be double—the double raw edges first being run onto the right side, and the fold being felled or slip hemmed to the garment on the wrong side just over the line of running, so that the stitches do not show on the right side.

Note that when the material is a stretchy one the joined-up strips should be stretched over the table edge before being sewn on, and especially if the edge being bound is on the inside of a curve, as on a round neck edge.

SCALLOPED EDGES

These are most attractive, and may be made in two ways: (*a*) bound with bias strips or (*b*) faced on the inside. For (*a*) see Fig. 106, p. 167, and the instructions on the same page; and for (*b*) see Fig. 107, p. 167, and the instructions on pp. 167–8. Note that when using (*b*) for lingerie the facing should be felled neatly instead of being slip hemmed, as the latter method is not firm enough to stand washing. If liked, a fancy stitch such as chain stitch may be worked on the right side over the felled stitches.

BUTTONHOLED SCALLOPS

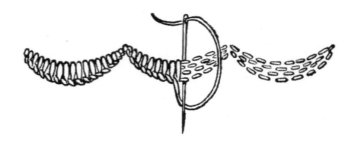

Fig. 144.—Buttonholed Scalloping.

These are quite suitable for a thin material if it is firm and does not fray easily, otherwise the result does not repay the time spent on the work, and the scallops pull out of shape in washing. A very thin fabric, even though firm, may be faced on the wrong side with material cut to the shape of the edge and about 1 inch deeper than the scallops. The outer edges should be tacked level, leaving as much as possible outside the scallops to give a good "hold" for working, and the other edge of the facing should be turned in and felled neatly. A transfer may be used to mark the scallops, or their shape may be cut in brown paper round a coin—four or five in a row—and then the scallops may be drawn on the material round this pattern. When going round a curve, either outer or inner, some adjustment of the paper will be needed, either cutting or pleating it above or below the scallops so that their shape is not altered.

First run finely along the outlines of the scallops, then fill in the spaces between with running stitches. When working with silk, the padding may be done with matching cotton for economy. This running, besides rounding out the covering stitches, prevents the material splitting between the scallops. Now work over the padding with loop stitch (usually, though not correctly, known as buttonhole stitch), as shown in Fig. 144, p. 268, taking the stitches from left to right. Press the scallops on the wrong side over a padded surface, then with a sharp-pointed pair of scissors cut away the material outside the scallops from the back, being most careful not to cut the stitches.

FACED EDGES

When the edges are on the curve, hems are difficult, and facings are often substituted. If a different colour is used, they can be most decorative, as the second colour may be allowed to peep just 1/12 inch or 1/8 inch beyond the edge of the garment. Cut out the facing strips in the way described for bound edges, but when the edges are irregular it is best not to stretch the strips before applying them. Instead, when sewing the strip to an inner curve—for instance, a round neck curve—ease the strip very slightly, then turn the strip over and tack the edges level, stretching the other edge of the strip to allow it to fit the material below. If the edge of the facing is to project a little, then the strip must not be eased. When you are setting a facing on the outside of a curve, stretch the edge a little as you run it on, then, after turning the strip over onto the wrong side, you may need to ease it a little on the lower edge, or even to make tiny pleats here and there, to make the facing fit the diminishing width. But when the edge to be faced is very much curved or very irregular is is best to tack a piece of material to the right side of it, the two matching in grain, and with right sides together; then, after running round the outside edges, the facing should be turned to the inside of the garment and cut to an even depth before turning in and felling the raw edge.

APPLIED NET EDGES

First Method

For this it is necessary that the outside edges of the net should be straight, although the depth of the strip need not necessarily be equal all round. It is best to draw on paper the shape of the garment, and then mark on this the shape the net edge is to take. For instance, the garment edge may be applied to net in scallops in the following way. Stamp or draw the scallops on the material, and allow enough net to be fourfold and to go under the scallops with 1/2 inch to spare. Fold the net once, then again, and make the fold meet the cut edges— it is now fourfold. Place the double fold to the outside edge marked on the paper and tack finely to the paper. Now lay the scalloped edge over the net, allowing as much net as you like beyond the scallops. Tack the material to the net and the paper, then run round the scalloped outlines through both material and net, using embroidery cotton or silk in accordance with the materials. Work the scallops as described for buttonholed scallops in Fig. 144.

Second Method

Here also the edge of the net should be on the straight thread, although the edge to which it is to be applied may be quite straight or very slightly curved. The finished width of the net should not be more than 3/4 inch. Fold the net as before to make it fourfold, but when folding the second time let the raw edges project 1/8 inch beyond the fold, then turn them in and tack them level with the folded edge. Draw the shape of the garment edge on to brown paper, and from this measure the width of the net strip and draw a second line. Now tack the net to the paper, and when going round a curve stretch the net edge very slightly. Tack the other edge also. (This stretching should only be slight, as otherwise, when washed, the net will go to its original shape and the effect will be spoiled. If the curve is very marked, tiny pleats should be made and sewn to the neck.)

EMBROIDERY

ALL the stitches needed for embroidering any material you may choose for your lingerie are described fully in *Teach Yourself Embroidery*, but it is well to remember that adaptation to the nature of the fabric is often necessary. For instance, when working on fine lawn, the embroidery thread must be fine and the stitches tight and well padded; while when using silk or crêpe-de-chine, a fairly coarse embroidery silk may be employed, and the designs may be freer in style, and not worked so finely. Though here, again, one must always consider future washings, and therefore not use stitches which may be disarranged easily either during this process or in the subsequent ironing.

FAGGOTING

Faggoting gives scope for originality in the trimming of lingerie—yokes, cuffs, neck edges, etc. It consists in joining together strips of material, ribbon, or lace insertion by means of fancy stitches, of which there is a great variety from which to choose.

First draw out on stiffish paper the shape you require the faggoting to be, but leave a few inches of spare paper all round.

Now draw out the design on the paper. This may consist simply of bands following the shape of the outside edge of the paper, or it may be an arrangement of bands twisting and turning, leaving somewhat irregular spaces. But the width of the bands, varying from 1/4 inch or less to 1/2 inch, should be the same throughout the design.

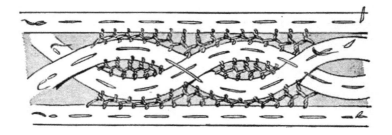

Fig. 145.—Simple Border in Faggoting.

In Fig. 145, below, you see a simple design for neck or sleeve edges; and, though the edge bands are shown on the straight, they may be adapted easily to a slight curve by stretching one edge of the strip as you tack it into place. The bands here consist of bias strips of crêpe-de-chine 3/8 inch wide, although the width is just a matter of taste. Cut out the strips as previously described, making them twice the desired finished width plus 1/4 inch for turnings. Join up the strips on their straight edges, press the turnings open, then fold the long strip with right side inside and raw edges meeting. Machine these raw edges together with 1/8-inch turnings. Now attach a bodkin (or small safety-pin) to the seam at one end of the strip, leaving about 3 inches of double thread when joined on. Turn the bodkin back and insert it in the casing. Push it along until you have turned out the strip completely and the bodkin emerges at the other end. (A similar method of turning a bias fold is illustrated on p. 172 in Figs. 111 A and B, though there a large safety-pin is used for a wider fold.) Now arrange the seam to come in the middle of what will be the under side, and press lightly with a warm iron on this side.

Tack the band to the paper in the position you have drawn out for it. One row of rather fine tacking-stitches is sufficient for a narrow band, but when wider than 3/8 inch, and when going round curves, both edges must be tacked. In this case the outer edge of the strip must be stretched slightly, and on the inner edge it may sometimes be necessary, though not always, to gather finely and draw up the thread to fit the curve. Sometimes it is better to make a tiny pleat instead of gathering, especially for a sharply-pointed corner. Now work across the spaces with the stitch D shown in Fig. 146, p. 276, though any one of the stitches shown in this Fig. may be used.

The thread used should be (for silk materials) twisted silk of the kind made specially for embroidering lingerie; for mercerised goods or plain cotton, tightly-twisted mercerised threads serve very well. A firm start should be made for the connecting stitch with a few tiny back stitches on the under side of the strip, and great care should be taken not to draw the stitches tightly, as even when they do not appear tight while the strips are on the paper they may do so when the strips are removed, so this fact should be borne in mind. As a rule the work is removed after all the strips have been joined, and is then neatened at the back and pressed; but at other times it is advisable to keep it tacked to the paper and attach the faggoting to the garment in that position. One's own discretion must be used as to which is the better plan in any particular case.

Faggoting Stitches

Four very useful connecting stitches are shown in Fig. 146, though it is an easy matter to find or invent others equally suitable.

A. Join on the thread at the right hand at the back of the lower strip. Bring out the needle at the front just below the folded edge.* Insert the needle in the upper strip, from the point exactly opposite where the thread came out on the lower strip; draw out the needle to leave a rather loose stitch, then pass it under the stitch thus made three times, and bring out in the lower strip close to where the thread came out, but slightly to the right. Draw up the thread, but not tightly, then insert the needle where it just came out and pass it along the inside of the fold from 1/4 to 1/2 inch to the left (according to the width of the strips), then repeat from*.

B. Join on the thread at the right hand in the lower strip,* take the thread straight across to the upper strip, and pass the needle to the back; bring out again in the same edge about 1/8 inch to the left. Take a straight stitch across to the lower strip and insert in the edge 1/8 inch from the first stitch. Pass the needle along the back and bring out 1/8 inch to the left. Repeat from*. Bear in mind that these straight stitches must be decidedly loose and must be spaced perfectly evenly. When the whole length has been done carry the needle to the middle of the end stitch and fasten there, then turn the work so that the stitches are horizontal. Hold the thread coming from the fastening under the left thumb just below the first three stitches. Insert the needle to the left of the thread above the top stitch and pass the point under the three stitches, bringing it out over the thread which is held under the thumb. Draw up the thread tightly to form a knot. Then repeat over groups of three stitches. Here again do not draw the thread tightly between the knots, or the finished effect will be ruined.

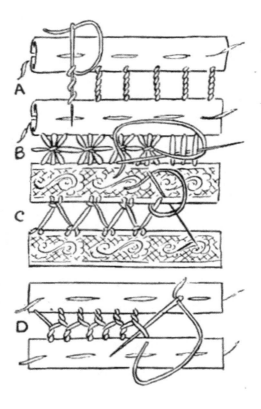

Fig. 146.—Some Faggoting Stitches.

C. Work this with the strips running downward. Join on the thread at the top of the left strip, and bring out on the upper side about 1/16 inch from the edge if a fabric strip is being used, or just inside the corded edge if insertion is employed. Hold the thread under the left thumb about 3/4 inch below where it came out, insert the needle in the same edge about 1/16 inch below where the thread came out, and bring out through the loop of thread. Garry the thread across slantingly to the other strip, and insert the needle about 3/16 inch below the level of the stitch on the other side, and here make two little loops, as shown. Then carry the thread to the left strip at the same slant as before and repeat the two little loop stitches. Repeat as required. The beauty of this stitch lies in the regular slanting of the crossing threads.

D. Work this with the strips running across. Join thread to the left end of the upper strip, bringing out the needle on the upper side.* Carry the thread across to the lower strip about 1/8 inch farther on to the right, pass the needle under it and bring out on the upper side. Pass the needle under the crossing thread from right to left, then insert under the upper edge about 1/4 inch from where the first stitch was inserted, and bring out on the upper side. Pass the needle under the crossing thread from right to left as before, then repeat from*, keeping the stitches spread regularly.

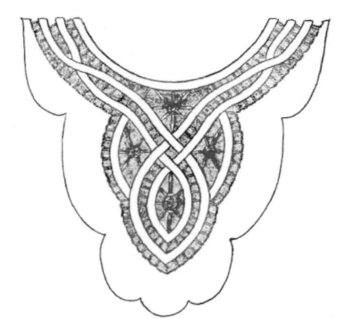

Fig. 147.—Dainty for Nightdress or Petticoat.

A More Elaborate Design (Fig. 147)

This makes a charming trimming for the front neck of a nightdress or petticoat-slip of crêpe-de-chine or satin. The strips are 3/16 inch wide when finished, and are prepared in the usual way. The spaces are irregular in shape, and the connecting stitches must be adapted to suit them, being made longer and shorter, closer together or wider apart, as required.

34

The joining stitch is that shown in Fig. 146 A, and when a large space occurs it is filled in with a spider web.

After the stitchery has all been done, the work should be pressed lightly on the back through the paper. The edge of the garment should next be cut to shape and prepared for attaching. It should be noted that allowance should be made for a space of from to 3/16 to 1/4 inch between garment and trimming, and also that even when the garment appears to be set on plainly to the trimming, as in this case, yet really it should be allowed with a very slight fullness, or, when set on, it will appear skimpy. The garment edge should be hemmed very finely, or rolled and whipped. The edge should then be tacked to the paper, leaving the required space between it and the edge of the trimming.

In cases where a full edge is to be attached to the faggoting it should be rolled and whipped and drawn up to fit the faggoting with the required space left, and then tacked on carefully. After the connecting stitches have been worked (either the same as in the example or any other preferred), the faggoting should be removed from the paper and the under side made neat. All ends of thread should be fastened oft, crossed bands should be made firm, and any raw edges turned in and felled neatly into place. Then the trimming should be pressed lightly on the wrong side.

Pinched Strips (Fig. 148)

These are very decorative, but bands must not be more than 3/8 inch in width before being "pinched" After cutting and joining up the strips in the usual way, press them so that the join comes at one side. Join on the thread (usually the same as will be used for the faggoting) at the right end of the band; pass the needle and thread along the inside of the band and* bring out in the middle of it on the upper side, about 1/2 inch to the left. Then put the needle behind the band from the top and bring it out below the edge; hold the thread coming from the hole under the left thumb and carry it under the point of the needle from left to right. Now with the right hand draw up the thread tightly through the loop. Put back the needle through the knot thus made, pass it along the inside of the band, and repeat from*. Note that the knots should be drawn tightly, but the thread between them should be left easy.

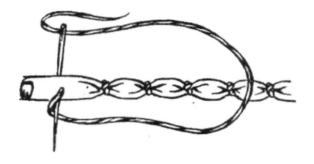

Fig. 148.—Making a Pinched Strip.

LINGERIE

APPLIQUÉ

Appliqué makes charming trimmings, which are at the same time durable, on crêpe-de-chine and other materials of fine, even weave, especially when two pale shades are used together—for instance, pink on blue, or mauve on pink, etc. The designs should be simple and have smooth, not serrated, edges, as the former are better for washing and wear. The usual methods of appliqué are described in *Teach Yourself Embroidery*, but it is well to remember that for lingerie the stitches should be small, even, and set closely together—

preferably buttonhole stitch or padded satin stitch. But there is another method which may be described here, which, while not strictly appliqué, produces a similar effect.

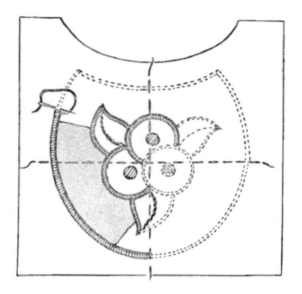

Fig. 149.—Appliqué Trimming for Lingerie.

In Fig. 149, p. 281, you see a trimming which could be used for front neck of petticoat-slip or nightdress or for nightdress sleeves or the sides of knickers. A motif of the same material as the garment rests upon a background of similar material, but in another colour, or of white or cream net, and is enclosed in a line of buttonhole stitch to form a circle, shield, or other suitable shape. You can easily draw such a design yourself, using a penny as a guide for the three circular flowers, and drawing the leaves freehand ; or, if you prefer it, it is easy to buy a similar transfer. If you use one of these, iron it off on to the garment in the desired position ; but if you draw your own design, outline it with a fine pencil on tracing paper, then lay a piece of carbon paper in the correct position for the design and place the tracing paper over the carbon. Trace the outlines with a hard, firm pencil, and be most careful that your fingers do not press over the carbon, or irremovable marks will be made. (In the case of new carbon papers, some of the colouring matter should first be removed with a soft rag or tissue paper.)

If you are using the same material, but of a different colour, for the background, cut a piece large enough to cover the outside edges of the space and with a spare 2 inches all round it. Be sure to match the garment material in weave. If you are using net, cut it in the same way, but double. Whichever you use, place it *under* the design on the garment, allowing an equal margin all round the outside line. Tack to the garment first from top to bottom, then from side to side, then tack again at each side of the first line at a distance of 1 inch; then again twice across, equally spaced. Finally run together round the outside line rather finely.

Now work round the outlines of all parts of the motif in tight buttonhole stitch over one or two lines of fine running in the embroidery thread, keeping the corded edge to the outside. Be careful to take all stitches right through both layers of material. Use fine corded silk for silk materials or twisted cotton for cotton goods. (This should match the material of the garment in colour.) When all this has been done work round the enclosing line in the same way, but with the corded edge of the stitch on the inside. Work the ribs of the leaves in outline stitch, and the roundels in the middle of the flowers in padded satin stitch. Then take a pair of fine-pointed scissors and cut away the material (upper only) between the motif and the enclosing buttonholing, as in Fig. 149. Press lightly on the wrong side.

LACE TRIMMINGS

These may be in the form of medallions, motifs, edging, insertion, etc. In any case, choose strong lace which will last as long as the garment, otherwise much labour is expended in renewing the trimmings while the garment itself is still in good condition. How to apply medallions, edging, and insertion is described on pp. 173–4 under the heading Lace. You will find an illustration of the second method of applying insertion in Fig. 150 A and B. Here note that at the crossing of the insertion the under piece is cut away and the raw edges are turned back and run to the upper piece, but when the lace is very fine this is not necessary.

There are also very attractive machine-made laces of artificial silk on net in white, ecru, and colours. They include yokes, motifs, neck and sleeve trimmings, etc., and are suitable for use on any of the silk (real or artificial) fabrics sold for lingerie. To attach them, lay the garment, right side upward, on a flat surface and place the lace over it, also right side upward. Pin together in many places, then tack carefully, and be sure not to get either lace or garment tight upon the other. Take silk matching the lace in colour, and work tiny stitches from the material over the edge of the lace. These stitches should be very close together and as small as possible. After this has been done turn to the back and cut off the turnings to 1/8 inch or less. Oversew the raw edges, or loop stitch them, to prevent fraying, or, if preferred, turn them under and fell very finely to the lace.

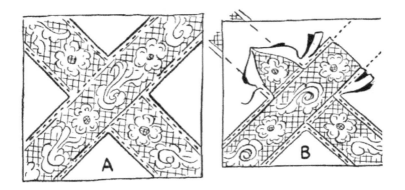

Fig. 150A and B.—Applying Insertion.

A   B

Right Side.   *Wrong Side.*

EMBROIDERY EDGINGS AND INSERTIONS

When the edging is narrow and is to be set onto the garment plainly—for instance, on the edge of the round neck of a nightgown—it is usual to place a beading between the edging and the garment. The beading can be set on as described in Chapter XX for a beaded seam (see Fig. 140, p. 262, and Fig. 151 on this page). When there is no material left on the beading, place the beading right side downward on the right side of the material, with the latter projecting about 1/8 inch above the corded edge. Then roll this little turning toward you over the corded edge and whip the two together the reverse way—that is, with the beading facing you and the material turning rolled over the corded edge.

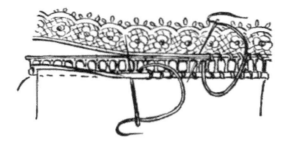

Fig. 151.—Applying Beading and Edging.

To apply the embroidery edging to the beading, cut off the required amount of plain material, then proceed as just described. In Fig. 151 the edging is lace, so the work is even simpler, and the needle is inserted from the back instead of from the front.

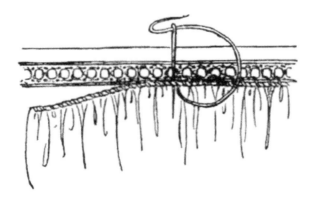

Fig. 152.—Whipping Fullness to Beading or Insertion.

When setting on beading to full material, the latter should be rolled and whipped as described on p. 58, then the two must be whipped together as in Fig. 152.

Applying Embroidery Insertion

There are at least three ways of applying embroidery insertion.

A. If the insertion is to have plain material at each side, place the embroidery with right side to right side of the material, and run together finely. Then cut off the turning of the garment to 1/16 inch, and that of the insertion to a thread or two more. Roll over the two edges towards you, and then use the needle as in Fig. 153. The other edge of the insertion may be applied to plain material in the same way, or may be whipped to beading or edging as before described for beading.

Fig. 153.—Applying Embroidery Insertion to Plain Edge.

B. When the insertion has a corded edge, cut off the plain material close up to it, then tack the insertion with its right side to that of the material; but leave a little turning of the latter above the insertion. Roll this turning toward you over the insertion and whip together in the usual way.

C. Enclose the insertion in a French seam. Place the wrong sides of insertion and material together and run or machine them just under 1/4 inch from the insertion edge. Cut off turnings as far as is safe, turn to wrong side, and run or machine close up to the insertion edge.

PICOTING

First read the paragraph on this subject on p. 175. It is possible to have almost the whole of a garment made at the machine shop—seams and hems being hemstitched, and any frills and neck and sleeve edges finished with picoting. This is quite satisfactory when very thin fabric such as ninon is in use. The seams must first be tacked, but not as for hand-sewing. One edge should be laid flat over the other as shown in Fig. 141A, and a line of tacking made through the two fitting-lines. If the lower edge is to be picoted, the line for this must be tacked, leaving at least 2 inches below. But if there is to be a hemstitched edge, this cannot be done until the seams have been treated, and so a second visit to the machine shop will be necessary. Any edges, such as those of frills, must be tacked along the fitting-line; turnings of from 1 1/2 to 2 inches should be left, and where any edges are much curved they should be tacked onto tissue paper. But if a good length of frilling is needed and a large piece of material is available, a simpler way is to measure the frilling on this with a ruler, so as to get the exact depth, and to tack the dividing lines finely. The stitch will be worked on these lines, and all that will be needed is to cut through the stitching.

When the garment returns, cut off the seam turnings on both sides as close to the stitching as possible, but on any outside edges cut through the middle of the stitching. Hems may be tacked with either a single or a double turn. If the former, then tack up at an even height all round above the lower edge of the garment, leaving a turning of at least 1 inch above the tacked line; if the latter, make the two turns of the same depth when the fabric is transparent, then tack close to the turned-in edge; but when the fabric is not transparent, the raw edge should be turned in for at least 1/4 inch. The hemstitching will then come half on the hem and half on the single material. One thing should always be remembered— that is, always to tack for hemstitching or picoting with matching thread, as it will be caught in with the machining and cannot be removed.

TUCKS

Full directions for making several varieties of tucks are given on pp. 153–6, and any one of these is suitable for lingerie, with the exception of corded tucks. Tucks are often alternated with lace or embroidery insertion with good effect.

PLEATS

These are not used much for lingerie, except for the fullness which is often placed in the side seams of petticoat-slips to give ease for walking and yet at the same time preserve a slim outline. Inverted pleats are most suitable here, and they are described on pp. 161–2.

GATHERS

Read the instructions for gathers on p. 166. Note that most of the materials now in vogue for lingerie are sufficiently supple to allow the stroking stitch to be dispensed with, though this is necessary with the old-fashioned stout fabrics such as long-cloth or cambric. This stroking, when it must be used, is worked in the following way.

Mark off the edge to be gathered in quarters to correspond with similar marks on the band or edge to which the gathers are to be joined. Then gather on the fitting-line (see Fig. 25, p. 56). A second row of gathers *above* the first makes them set better. Draw up the threads fairly tightly and twist them round a pin which is set in point downward at the left end. Hold the gathers in the left hand, and with the eye of a coarse sewing-needle or the blunt end of a wool needle press each little fold into place against the thumb of the left hand, working from left to right. This stroking must be done very gently, and on no account should the sharp point of a needle be used, or the material will be scratched and its surface ruined. Stroke in the same way on the wrong side, then let out the gathers to the required width.

Setting Gathers into a Band

When setting gathers of stout material into a waist-band or sleeve-cuff, etc., proceed as follows:

The waist- or sleeve-band will be cut out with the warp threads running round the figure for strength. If the band is to be in the form of a ring, join up the ends on the wrong side and press the turnings open; if the ends are to be open, fold the band down the middle on the wrong side and join up each end. Now in either case turn up 1/4 inch or less on each edge of the band. Quarter the band and mark with pins, then match up with the quarterings on the gathered edge, and pin together there. Lay the turned-up edge of the band over the gathers on the right side so that the lower gathering thread is just covered. First pin into place, then tack finely through the folded edge. Now fell the folded edge between the gathers— one stitch to each gather—producing upright stitches. When finished, turn to the wrong side and tack in the same way, except that the fold should come the slightest bit higher than on the right side in order that the second set of felling stitches will not show through on the right side.

When Using the Sewing Machine

After letting out the gathers to the desired width, take the band and crease one edge only; then lay this right side downward on to the right side of the gathers and tack very finely through band and gathers on the creased line, which should come exactly over the lower gathering thread. Now turn the garment to the wrong side and turn up the band on the lower edge; then tack it over the gathers with the fold just a shade below the fold on the right side. Now stitch from the right side close to the fold of the band; and if the ends are open, then carry the stitching up the ends also.

For Very Thin Fabrics

For the thin fabrics, now generally used, the gathers are usually set into bands similarly to the method used for machining just described, but with a fine running stitch over the first row of tacking (before the band is turned up), and felling on the wrong side, as for the hand-sewn method. But when the fullness is set onto a single edge it must be done by rolling and whipping.

Waist Fullness at Side of Petticoat

In a princess petticoat or slip there is often a horizontal cut on the waist-line at each side of the under-arm seam, into which fullness on the lower edge is set. Stitch the side (under-arm) seams as you prefer—usually French seams—then take two bias strips of the same material 3/4 inch wide. Place one strip on the upper side of the cut with right sides together and raw edges level; tack the two together. Turn to the wrong side and tack the other strip over the cut in the same way, then run or machine together as close to the raw edges as is safe (see Fig. 154A). Gather the lower edge to fit the upper, then turn in the edge of the strip on the right side and tack it over the gathers. Fell this into place by hand, or machine close to the turned-up edge (see Fig. 154B). Tack down the strip on the wrong side in the same way and fell into place (see Fig. 154C).

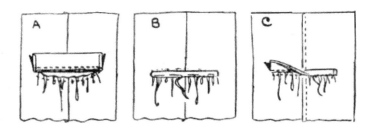

Fig. 154.—Waist Fullness at Side of Petticoat.

SMOCKING

This may often be employed in lingerie, particularly when the gathering is fine and the fancy stitches firm and close, so that they do not get disarranged in washing. (Smocking, of course, is always in favour for children's frocks, and from time to time it is fashionable for blouses for adult wear.)

The amount of fullness required for smocking varies with the thickness and texture of the material, and also with the stitches to be used. The average amount required is three times the width of the finished measurement, but thicker materials will not need so much fullness, and very fine ones can take more.

Preparation

The preparation of the material for the fancy stitching, by means of rows of gathers, is all-important. To ensure perfect regularity there are two methods.

1st Method. Buy a transfer of rows of evenly-spaced dots. On fine materials the dots should be from 1/4 inch to 3/8 inch apart, while on thicker ones 1/2 inch is usual. See to it that the top edge of the material is cut by a thread. Place the transfer on the *wrong* side of the material with the rows of dots on the straight thread.

Calculate how many rows of gathers you will need for the fancy stitches and add one extra for the top row, which will usually be set into a band of some kind. Tack the paper into place on the *wrong* side of the material with the row of dots on the same thread, then apply a hot iron.

2nd Method. Take a ruler and pencil or chalk and rule horizontal lines the required distance apart, keeping on the straight thread. Now cross these lines with downward ones to form perfect squares.

The Gathering (Fig. 155)

This is done on the wrong side with fairly thick but soft cotton. Make a large knot on the cotton, which cannot be pulled through the fabric. Now begin at the right hand by taking a stitch under a few threads exactly on the dot or at the crossing of the lines on the squares. Continue to the end of the row, and here cut the cotton, leaving about 1 inch. Repeat until all the rows have been gathered, then make an extra row about 1/8 inch above the top row, taking up the threads immediately above the stitches of the row below. (This extra row gives firmness.) Now draw up two threads at once from the left hand and twist them together round a pin placed vertically at the end of the two rows. Repeat until all the rows are drawn up to an equal width (Fig. 156). This should be almost as much as the desired finished width.

Fig. 155.—Foundation Gathering for Smocking.

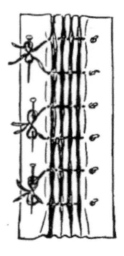

Fig. 156.—Drawing up the Gathers.

Planning the Stitches

It is necessary to have a clear plan in your mind before beginning the fancy stitches. This can then be drawn out on squared paper and consulted as you work. Almost any fancy embroidery stitch can be used—most usually outline, crewel, feather, chain, etc.—and some of the elaborate patterns are simply arrangements of one or two stitches in diamonds or waved lines. They are not difficult to carry out, but they entail careful counting of stitches and folds on the material so that a whole pattern, or else the division between two patterns, comes in the exact middle of the finished work.

Holding the Work

The material may be held in the left hand while being worked, or it may be tacked carefully to a piece of stout but pliable paper, and then the gathers should be stretched out to the exact width desired. Some stitches are worked from right to left, some from left to right, and for some others—such as chain stitch—the work must be turned so that the little folds come horizontally and the stitch is worked downward.

Fig. 157

This is a simple pattern to start with, being merely an arrangement of crewel, outline, and chain stitches. Ten rows of gathers are required, with an extra row worked 1/8 inch above the top row for strength. These two will not be worked on. Work a row of crewel stitch on the second and fourth gathered rows, and a row of chain stitch on the third row of gathers. Repeat these on the eighth, ninth, and tenth rows of gathers. In the space left work a trellis band as follows:

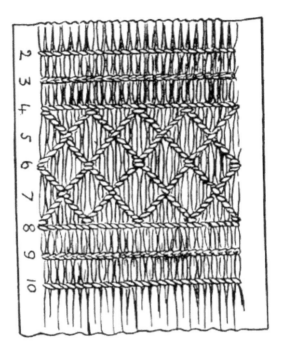

Fig. 157.—A Simple Pattern for a Start.

Begin close up to the straight row of crewel stitch at the left hand. Bring out the needle to the left of a fold and* work outline stitches in a slanting row, making the fifth stitch exactly on the fifth gathered row, and bringing out the needle after the ninth stitch exactly on the sixth gathered row. Now work nine crewel stitches slanting upward to the straight crewel row. Repeat from*. Next start with a stitch on the sixth gathered row exactly underneath the first stitch of the previous slanting row of stitches. Now work a slanting row of crewel stitches to the fourth gathered row, immediately in the middle of the space. Then continue working downward and upward to cross the previous rows of stitches to form diamonds and triangles. Now repeat what has just been worked on the sixth, seventh, and eighth gathered rows.

Here is a reminder that when working outline stitch horizontally from left to right the needle is brought out *below* the previous stitch, while when working the same vertically the needle is brought out to the *right* of the previous stitch. But when working crewel stitch horizontally the needle is brought out *above* the previous stitch, while when working vertically it is brought out to the *left* of the previous stitch.

The border is finished with three rows to match the upper part of the border—a row of crewel stitch on the eighth and tenth gathered rows, and a row of chain stitch on the ninth gathered row.

Fig. 158

Eight gathered rows are needed for this pattern, adding an extra row for firmness immediately above the top row—neither of these being worked over, and not being shown in the diagram. Work over the second and fourth gathered rows in crewel stitch, or outline, if preferred, and work over the third gathered row in single feather stitch.* Join the thread at the left hand close to the last row of crewel stitch, and bring out the needle to the left of a fold. Work five slanting outline stitches down to the next (the fifth) gathered row; then work upward to the fourth gathered row with five crewel stitches. Repeat from* as required. (See that the triangles thus formed are equally spaced.) Now join on to the beginning of the fifth gathered row and work as before between this and the sixth row, and when this is done work another row midway between the last two rows. After this join the thread on the seventh gathered row immediately under the first stitch on the fifth gathered row and work three waved rows as before, but in reverse, so as to form a row of diamonds between the two sets of three. Exactly in the middle of each diamond catch the two middle pleats together with two back stitches; finish off each pair of stitches separately so that the thread is not carried across at the back.

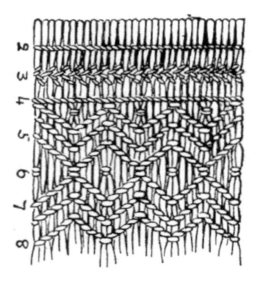

Fig. 158.—Waved Lines are Effective.

Honeycombing

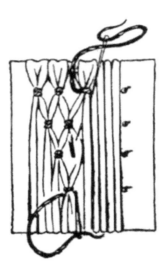

Fig. 159.—How to Work the Honeycombing.

This is the most elastic stitch of any used in smocking, and it may be used entirely by itself or combined with others. Fig. 159 shows exactly how it is worked. Bring out the needle to the left of a fold at the left hand of the work on the second gathered row. Take two back stitches over this fold and over the one to the right of it, and when making the second stitch insert the needle downward through the fold to the next gathered row, bringing it out there to the left of the second fold (which will be the first of the second pair). Now catch together this fold and the one to the right, as in the previous stitch, but in the last stitch pass the needle upward to the previous gathered row and bring it out to the left of the fold. (Both these movements are shown in Fig. 159.) Repeat these stitches on the two gathered rows alternately. To work subsequent rows repeat on the gathered rows below, either in the whole width of the material or in sets of diminishing stitches to form a vandyke pattern as in Fig. 160.

Fig. 160

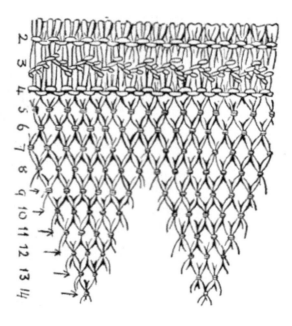

Fig. 160.—Honeycombing in Points.

Fourteen gathered rows are required for this, with an extra one just above the first—these two are not worked on, and are not shown in the diagram.

Work cable stitch over the second and fourth rows. This is similar to crewel stitch, but the needle is brought out above and below the previous stitch alternately. Work double feather stitch over the third gathered row. Honeycombing is worked over the next four gathered rows right across, and then the points are formed over the remaining six gathered rows.

Embroidery Threads

For lingerie it is well to choose a rather tightly twisted silk or cotton, with its thickness in proportion to the texture of the material. Stranded cotton may frequently be used, with the number of strands appropriate to the pattern and fabric. A fine crewel needle is the best to work with.

Finishing Off

After all the fancy stitches have been worked, and before taking out the gathering threads, place the work on an ironing blanket with wrong side upward. Pin out the edges straight, then place a damp cloth over the back of the work and pass the iron lightly over it. On no account press the work, or the whole effect will be spoiled. Then remove the damp cloth and hold the iron over the material, but not touching, until the steam has evaporated. Leave for a few minutes, and then withdraw the gathering threads. This process sets the gathers and gives a professional look to the work.

FASTENINGS

BUTTONS and buttonholes or buttons and loops are the most usual fastenings for lingerie. Hooks and eyes are taboo, and although press studs are sometimes seen on crêpe-de-chine and satin slips and petticoats, these neat little fastenings are frowned upon by experts on account of their unsuitability for washing.

Buttons and Buttonholes

Buttons for lingerie are generally either small pearl ones or small unpierced linen ones—the latter for lawn and cotton fabrics. The pierced linen ones are never used on dainty garments, and in any case buttons should always be as small as efficiency permits, for large ones are both clumsy and out of place, and are calculated to mar the beauty of an otherwise attractive and well-made garment. The buttons should be sewn into position before the holes are cut, or their positions should be marked with pencil or cross stitches, and the spaces between should be measured carefully with a ruler. (When many buttonholes are to be made, it is a good thing to space the positions out on cardboard and thus make a gauge to cut them by.) Buttons and buttonholes should, with very rare exceptions, always be on double material, and when there are several in line, as for instance on front, back, or side fastenings, the edges should either be hemmed back or faced with a strip of self-material. When the buttons and buttonholes are isolated, so that neither hem nor facing is practicable, a small square of material cut on the same grain as the button or buttonhole site should be placed beneath it and felled all round.

Use strong double silk or cotton, according to the material, for sewing on buttons. First make two small back stitches on the button site on the right side of the material, then place the button exactly over them and bring up the needle and thread through one of the holes in the button. Place a pin across the button and take the stitches over it. When there are four holes, make a cross of two stitches each way; if there are two holes, make four stitches across, then pass the needle to the back of the button, between it and the material; withdraw the pin and twist the thread three or four times round the sewing-on stitches to form a "neck". Pass the needle to the back, make one or two back stitches and cut the thread (see Fig. 71, p. 123).

For Shank or Covered Buttons

Moulds are sometimes covered with a circle of the garment material—this being gathered round the edge and drawn up into the centre of the under side. For these, and for buttons with a shank, the method of sewing is to start as before with small back stitches, then to pass the needle through the shank (or through the gathered covering of a mould), and then through the material and back again, repeating this as required for strength. In the case of a covered button a "neck" should be made as described for the button with holes.

For Linen Buttons

When linen (unpierced) buttons are used, begin work on the button site with two back stitches, then place a pin across the button and bring the needle out on the top. Carry the single thread four times over the pin and across a little space not more than one-third the width of the button and exactly in the middle of it; then bring the thread to the right side, remove the pin, and work loop stitch over the strands (as shown in Fig. 76, p. 129); make a "neck" as before, and secure the end of the thread.

Buttonholes

These are like those used in dressmaking, but not in tailoring. When the buttons have been sewn on, place the buttonhole side of the opening over them and mark the place of each button with a pin. Now either chalk or pencil the line for each buttonhole, using a ruler. The buttonholes should be on the straight thread, if possible, though this cannot always be managed, and if not, care must be taken that the slits are not stretched, and to prevent this it is wise to overcast the slit very lightly. The length of the slit should be 1/16 inch more than the width of the button, if this is a flat one; if it is a dome-shaped one, then 1/8 inch more. (But it is a good plan to cut experimental slits in a spare piece of material to make sure.) The distance of the buttonholes from the edge of the material should be enough to allow 1/8 inch, at least, beyond the buttons when they are fastened, so that this all depends on their size. Cut each slit as required, to avoid stretching.

Method of Working

Coarser thread than is used for the sewing of the garment should be employed for the buttonholes, and silk on all materials except cotton ones. (See Fig. 73, p. 127, for method.) Stitches should be as short as is compatible with strength, and they should be placed closely together with not more than a hair's breadth between them. The thread should be drawn up tightly to make a good knot after each stitch, and so that this knot comes exactly on the edge of the slit; but it should not be drawn up *over-tightly*, or it will tear the fabric.

To begin, secure the thread at the left end (that farthest from the edge of the material). Bring out the thread there just below the cut and begin to work the stitches from left to right as shown. After inserting the needle, take the thread coming from its eye and draw it round under the point from the left side, then draw up the needle to form the knot. When you reach the other end fan out the stitches (five or seven), and continue along the other side until you reach the starting point. Here pass the needle into the slit and out again at the beginning of the first stitch you made. From there take two or three stitches across the end of the buttonhole and bring out the needle at the left hand again. Then work buttonhole stitch over these strands, keeping them free of the material. Pass the needle to the back and finish off there. When making buttonholes downward (as for the front fastening of a shirt blouse) both ends must be barred.

Buttons and Loops

When the material is not firm enough to serve as a foundation for buttonholes, loops should be used instead. The buttons should be sewn on as before, and the position of the loops marked accordingly on the other side of the opening. Sometimes (*a*) the loops are made just under the edges so that the buttons are covered, and at others (*b*) they are made on the extreme edge. You must make your own choice. In any case the right side should be hemmed or faced to make it double.

Method A

Attach the thread for the loop to the left end of the right side of the garment (holding the edge towards you). Bring out the thread for the loop just under the edge and carry a strand across the space for the loop, which should be the width of the button. Leave this strand very slightly loose from the material. Make a tiny stitch through the fabric, then carry the thread back again to the starting point and take a tiny stitch there. Now test the loop over the button arid adjust if necessary. Carry two more strands across in this way, and then work over them in loop stitch (see Fig. 76, p. 129). When you finish at the right-hand end you may fasten off there with a few tiny back stitches, or, if you have enough thread, you may pass the needle through the material and bring it out at the next position and repeat.

Method B

Work as before, but on the extreme edge. Note that when round or dome-shaped buttons are used a looser loop will be needed, but this can only be decided by experiment.

Cord Loops

These are made in the same way as for dressmaking (described on p. 128 and illustrated in Fig. 75), but with one slight difference—in lingerie the edge for the cord must be hemmed before the cord is sewn on.

CASINGS FOR ELASTIC

These are needed at the waist and knees of directoire knickers. When the edge is on the straight, tack a hem one-and-a-half times the depth of the elastic, and stitch by machine on both top and bottom of the hem—hand sewing is not firm enough. Make an opening for elastic, preferably by unpicking the little bit of seam in the hem at the centre-back of a waist edge, or at the inside seam of knee edge. Buttonhole the edges of the opening. When there is not sufficient material for a hem, or the edge is curved, cut a bias strip twice the width of the elastic. Turn down and press the edge of the garment, then do the same to the raw edge of the bias strip and tack it just below the turned-down edge of the garment. Arrange the opening to come at the ends of the strip at the place suggested for a hem. Turn back both ends of the strip and buttonhole them as before. Turn up the other edge of the strip and tack it into place, then stitch on both edges as near the turn as possible.

Inserting Elastic

Pin a small safety-pin to one end of the elastic and run it through the casing. Join the ends of elastic by overlapping them for 1/2 inch and sewing firmly all round. If there is a small placket in the garment the elastic must not be joined, but the left end should be turned back twice and have a button sewn on it. This will keep the elastic from running back. On the other end of the elastic a hem should be made, and a buttonhole loop made on its extreme edge to pass over the button. Each end of elastic must be secured to the garment with a few stitches, but it can be removed easily if it is not desirable to wash it. If strings are to be used instead of elastic, the casings are made in the same way.

Other Casings

Sometimes a small casing is needed on the waistline at the back of a petticoat or other garment. In this case a strip of material cut on the selvedge threads is necessary, and it should be twice the width of the elastic, tape or ribbon. Top and bottom edges should be turned down narrowly, and rather more at each end. Then the upper and lower edges should be tacked into place and machined close to the fold, but the ends should be left open. If only one string is used, pass it through the casing and sew it through the middle of the strip with an upright row of back stitch or else a large cross stitch. If two strings to cross are used, sew one to each end of the casing before it is applied, then lay the strings flatly over one another, and tack and stitch the casing into place with one string emerging at each end. Be sure to keep clear of the strings when you are machining.

BUTTONHOLED SLOTS FOR RIBBON

These slots are often used round the waist and neck of nightgowns and petticoats. They must of necessity be in single material, and so this must be firm, even though at the same time it may be fine. The slots are always upright, never horizontal. Draw them on the material with pencil and ruler. They should be inch longer than the width of the ribbon. They are usually in pairs about 1 inch apart, leaving about 2 inches between the pairs. The slots must be worked very lightly in buttonhole stitch, but without pulling tightly on the corded edge, and both ends must be the same—either barred or round. On very fine material—say lawn, crêpe-de-chine or silk—the slots may be whipped as in *broderie anglaise* in the following way: Pencil the slot, but do not cut it. Take needle and fine embroidery cotton for lawn, or twisted embroidery silk for silk, and run finely round the mark on both sides. Then cut the slit and work close over-and-over stitches from right to left all round over the running stitches, turning down the extreme edge with the needle as you go along.

SEWING ON STRINGS

If ribbon strings are to be set into the ends of hems, they should be sewn on before the hems are sewn. Arrange the hem, then tack the end of ribbon for 3/4 inch to the inside of the hem and stitch the hem. If hand-stitched, then the ribbon must be felled to the hem at each end, but if machined the line of stitching may be carried up the ends of the hems. When the ribbon is not to be in a hem, but sewn inside the ends of an opening, place the end of the ribbon—right side downward—about 3/4 inch from the end of the garment. Run the ribbon to the material, then turn the ribbon over and fold it backward to meet the edge of material. Seam the two together, and then flatten out the seam, after which fell the side edges of the ribbon.

SHOULDER STRAPS

Ribbon or double strips of the garment material are generally employed for the shoulder straps of cami-knickers, petticoats, etc., when these have straight-edged tops. Their position depends on the figure, and should be marked with pins after trying on the garment. Sew them on as described for ribbon strings. The stitches should not show on the right side, so, if the material is thin, it is best to make a small bow of ribbon, or a rosette, to cover any stitches.

Mark the position of the straps, then make a buttonhole slot (vertical) in the garment at each position. If the material is single, it must be backed with small pieces for strength, felling these finely all round. Hem each end of the ribbon and sew a flat button on the under side of each, covered on the right side with a bow or rosette. The button goes through to the inside of the garment.

To Prevent Straps Slipping

On the turnings of each shoulder seam of a frock attach a little strap of double material near the neck. Fasten the other end by means of press studs either to the turnings near the armhole seam, or to the end of the sleeve extender. Pass the petticoat straps under this little strap and you will be spared the discomfort of shoulder straps halfway down the arm.

Ingram Content Group UK Ltd.
Milton Keynes UK
UKHW040705170423
420292UK00001B/92